T0021683

The Sound
of
Falling Snow

JOHN RYAN

authorHOUSE®

AuthorHouse™ UK
1663 Liberty Drive
Bloomington, IN 47403 USA
www.authorhouse.co.uk
Phone: 0800.197.4150

Published by AuthorHouse 05/04/2018

ISBN: 978-1-5462-9261-6 (sc)
ISBN: 978-1-5462-9262-3 (hc)
ISBN: 978-1-5462-9260-9 (e)

Print information available on the last page.

Contents

Mental Illness amongst Friends

A word of wisdom to the wise concerning
Mental states amongst the many folk I met
As the moon shone on corridors in Bedlam's
Frozen wastes.

These poor souls were frozen out from humankind's
Kinder ways. We formed unsteady bonds, broken
When we left for good—or so we thought back then.
Incarcerated yet again in months, newer bonds were
Formed, endless cycles of enduring faith.

Mental illness is still a scourge, not least to those
Who're left behind to worry and to fret. I'll ne'er
Erase the memories of Bedlam's putrid ways. I simply
Can't comply with dictates from on high this hour. 'Get
A grip,' they say, but little do they know.

A constant state of torpor overcame these new-found
Friends. But they suffered all alone through the endless
Nights. The days were just the same. My soul went out
To them. I still recall the many talks we had. Today I
Wonder where they are, if they are safe from ill, and
Ill-informed comment amongst the literati of the world.

Bedlam must disintegrate; it serves no purpose but to
Cause the pain unique to friends of mine who're close
To me. Bedlam I did curse back then. Today I curse it yet
Again. 'It serves no good,' I say. 'Let them free,' I plead.

Roses Bloom in June

In my Garden of Delights, the roses bloom in June.
I sit and hear the sap and watch them gain more
Strength as days wear on in languid form, delightful
To the eye.

Geraniums are jealous, I do sometimes think.
Combined, they form the perfect scene in my secret
Garden space. No life without a garden, in my crazy
View.

But my roses lead the way, colours, hues eternal deep
Inside this poorly head of mine. They are my solace in
Old age. A heavy scent exuding now, I sniff and sniff.
Again, I can't resist this hour as summer nears its peak.

A rose forever in my hand, rose fever in my heart.
Better this year than the last, perfection now for me.
Sipping slowly, I doze off, contemplating roses grand.
My special time when roses grow, days dawdling in
The dizzy scent, my tablet spewing out my poems grand
And plentiful.

June and roses made for fun and happy thoughts of glee.
Summertime and roses time, time to spend composing
Verses varied that may just last.

The roses need some water now, but not until the sun
Is spent. Evening coolness just in time. I'm so arthritic
I can't manage it alone. The splashing water sound is
Heaven's gift to me. Tomorrow's roses all the more exotic,
Of this I'm sure.

A Loving Home

A loving home was all I knew as I
Grew up. We were lucky, I do think
This reflective hour.

Parents showering all their love
And caring all the while. Spoilt
Maybe, or some would say we
Imbibed it all without a care.

In later years, as I looked back, I
Looked with love at well-worn
Photos of those frugal times.
Happy us, not knowing worldly

Ways so nasty and so horrible.
Simple lives ensconced in nature.
Wild. A rural lifestyle all about
As we hunted foxes for our

Pleasure; mad. Growing up in
Kindness, we did take that to our
Brain somewhat. It has lasted to
This day, I guess.

It made us who we are.

As I Got Older

As I got older, I thought I had it all worked
Out. Life got in the way so suddenly.
Compromising quickly, the game of cat
And mouse became the norm.

First love shone bright so suddenly. I was
Besotted so, but not for long as these
Things go. Emotions compromised, I
Found a better second love to see with.

Newer eyes. Relationships were fickle.
Then so it remained the mainstay of
A life much compromised. Learning
Complicated lessons faster than before.

Telepathic love, it seemed to me, for
Stability was needed. Soon. I fell in love
In Poland fair; has lasted forty years.
Now the memories alone.

I Go to Church

I make my way to church more slowly.
Now eight thirty in the morn, while
Most folk lie indoors for yet another
Hour. I go to church to think of all
Those times in youth when such a
Burden was simply not a choice.

But now I'm working hard in church,
Praying too for all my friends in
Bedlam's grip this day. Reformed I'm
Not; I'm a rebel to the core. But pray
We must for humankind. I simply do
My bit humbly and with gratitude.

Energy's not wasted here. We join
Across the globe to lay before the
Lord one last request for deep,
Deep peace for each and every one.
Bedlam haunts me to this day, so
I pray for those incarcerated deeply
Within this hour.

No release for some of them. For
Those I pray especially. God grant
Them strength to cope. My weekly
Prayer does give me a deep sense
Of gratitude for mental strength
Alone at home. It's worth it just
For that.

The Sound of Falling Snow

Last night, ten billion flakes did float to celebrate.
Midwinter now, I cried within my breast at
Nature's sheer magnificence.

Ten billion is correct. I counted all of them as I'd
Overdrunk my wine. I loved the sheer
Magnificence. I cried again at Nature's ways so
Silently.

Such a show laid on for me, I donned my coat
With haste and ventured forth to celebrate a
Spectacle so rare. Mild outside and beautiful,
Three times I cried. Just loved this show.
Unique, the sound of falling snow was all mine
To enjoy.

I've seen this spectacle in places far and wide,
But none could match this here. I left a muffled
Sound behind as I returned home, the memory
Forever etched in my happy, happy brain.

Oh, the sound of falling snow!

Roma's Legacy

Married forty years, we love each other
Still. Still we fight, and still we love until
The very end.

I love my Roma very much, in deep love
All those years. That's Roma's legacy
To me. And I am happy still.

Roma, Roma …

My Many, Many Books

My library is vast, the books a great help
In this old, old age of mine. I'm always sifting
Through to find a gem or two.

They are close, familiar friends of mine and
Have been down the years. A consolation
Deep when I am in ill health. My books they
Serve me well. Without a quibble—ever.

These days I download to my tablet new, so
Much easier for arthritic hands. I wish I'd
Had a tablet all those years ago, but I don't
Visit bookshops when I'm walking past.

My money doesn't stretch too far; my
Pension's all I've got. In the summer early
Morning time, it's time to climb the steps and
Recover a lost gem. I read it over coffee in my
Garden of Delights, with a roll-up for added joy.

Books of poetry, philosophy, and on computers
Too. All sorts I find just staring out at me,
Begging to be fondled one more time this hour.
My wife, she tells me, 'Get some sleep!' But I ignore
Her now.

Devastated I would be if I should lose this
Treasure trove of mine. I'd want to leave this
World for good. My books, my books!

A Slow, Slow Walk

It's a hazy afternoon in Finchley now.
Summertime as well, and off I go to
Saunter round about and meet old
Friends. We share the gossip,
Rumours, and the like.

My feet don't carry me too far but
Far enough to greet and smile. I
Pet the local dogs; they know me
Well by now, ambling with my
Walking stick, having cappuccinos
One more time before it's time to go.

My daily slow, slow walk means
Everything to me. In touch, in touch
With all that's going on in my
Beloved Finchley fair.

A Springtime Walk

A slow, slow walk through
The springtime growth is
Medicine for me. My heart is
Calm; my soul it is at peace.
The local dogs and owners
Know me well. I return their
Greetings merrily. The woods
Are busy putting on their
Springtime garb after months
Of public nakedness. The
Trees are now as trees are
Meant to be. I sit and rest and
Eye the miracle before my eyes.
Winter's gaunt despair no longer
In my thoughts, I stroke a friendly
Dog. This is peace indeed.
Nature on the mend at last. On
My way back home, I call for
Coffee and my fag. I sit outside
And watch the passers-by. I
Promise I will make a poem when
I get home at last. Springtime in
My heart is peace, deep peace
Within.

Rest at Last

The day is done and now
It's time to lay me down
Quite still.

Hard labour making poems
Through the day-long
Heat. Now there's respite,

Rest at last, through the
Stilly night till dawn.
Then I'll scratch myself

Awake and greet a new
Day happily that I may
Sleep and not keep

Waking through the
Moonlit hours, with tea
And biscuits as an aid to

Concentrate my mind.
Dear Lord, grant me all-
Night sleep—I know this

Is a wasted wish this hour.
Exceptions do occur.
Grant me one, I plead.

Christmas Time

My special Christmas time:
All close friends they write

To me for Old Time's Sake.
They always will, I hope.

In fancy, I imagine us now
Gathered 'round

Singing sacred songs
And through the ether they

Do flow in unison with angel
Choirs and the tweeting

Of the birds. We have mulled
Wine and pies to round

The whole thing off. Then we
Negotiate the footpaths

Frozen fast, inch by inch in

The dismal dark of sacred
Nights, lit by Christmas

Lanterns glowing, blowing
In the wintry wind.

My Irish Soul

I read *The Irish Times*
Voraciously: it's my anchor
On the world.

*The Guardia*n too: the
Two of them fill my mind
With all I need to know.

Such detailed articles
Keep my mind from
Wandering too far.

Writing of such quality
Keeps my soul intact.
My tablet is my friend.

My motherland is close to
Me: I need to know now
How she fares.

Never will I break these
Bonds. We are forever
Bound. Such artistic

Acumen amazes me each
Time. My veins, they're
Filled with Irish blood

Of which I'm very proud.
They'll bury me in Irish
Soil. Amen. Amen.

A New Poem

I'm holding in my hands
A poem that's just been
Born.

It's crying out for
Readers. Little does it
Know how long the

Whimpers they will last
For want of readers—all
Life long.

So, so delicate, a newly-
Crafted poem. Such beauty,
Such few words

Plucked from the bosom of
The Muse, no less. I pray
It will be read, and read

Again. The whimpers they
Will stop. My poem will
Mature. My pen I can

Put down at last.

Winter

Winter won't relent its
Tighter, fiercer grip today
With sleety snow outside,

A biting wind to boot.
I wait for springtime thaw,
The pulse of nature

Moving on. Water puddles,
A sheet of ice in my
Garden of Delights.

Slippery underfoot, I tread
One step at a time—gingerly.
No coffee shop today, I tell

Myself. The robin is alert,
Bobbing to and fro, pecking
At my offerings.

My study warm and snug: One
Word upon the page,
Two, and three, and then

I'm off. The gods are kind
To me tonight. I'll have a
Glass of Baileys to help
Me on my way.

My Coffee Shop

The smell of roasted coffee
Beans in my coffee shop
Is pure delight just now.

I watch the world drop
By—the regulars know
Me well by now.

A big, big lie—they know
Me not at all, truth
Be told.

Coffee, amaretti: my
Sustenance this hour.
Thank the Lord for coffee

Shops—such help creating
Goodly reads, and making
Folk commune.

I pass an hour, then ramble
On, poetic notions in my
Sleepy head, by now.

Furtive glances at my peers,
I stroke their pets, and
Am glowing deep inside.

An Open Fire

The sad, sad song of humankind
Echoes through the air on nights
Like this, a cold and frosty New
Year's night abroad. Too old I am
To venture out. I sit before my
Blazing fire—mid-winter's mood
Is in my soul. I wish I had a
Labrador to pet, but I am not
Allowed: quite stupidly, I
Say, and say again. 'They need a
Lot of walking. Look, you're too
Frail,' I'm told. In younger years
I loved my Labrador. Such fond
Memories on wintry nights like
This. My fire is crackling,
Spitting wood. No TV for me.
Just me, my tablet, and thoughts
Of youthful jumps across the
Moors. An old man reminiscing
Before a blazing fire, pleading for
A dog to pet and stroke, but to
No avail.

Robert Frost

I'm reading Robert Frost again;
I find his words so comforting.
Frost is my close companion
Deep at night, my tablet's
Working overtime.

Give me Maya Angelou, give
Me Robert Frost as well, as
Close, close night-time
Friends this happy hour. We
Make a cheerful threesome,

So we do. Sincerity of soul is
What matters now, as I observe
The moon riding wintry night,
And I pour a coffee, reassuring
Sustenance for long hours

Spent perusing mighty minds
For simple souls like me. Oh!
Robert Frost, that I could have

Your gifts within my mind this
Goodly hour. I want in shady

Woods to walk with you and
Talk with you. We two could
Walk untrodden paths, saying
Very little—just happy in the
Walking and the talking too.

Thank you for your legacy to me.
You live where all dead poets do
Live—a sacred place which we can
Visit overnight even this very hour.
Give me comfort in your words.

This is my one request to you and
All the other poets I venerate this
Stormy night outside. Let me walk
The winter woods with you when
Tomorrow comes. Oh! To walk

The winter woods with you, I
Plead again. For we have much in
Common now—kindred spirits
Strolling slowly on. I salute you,
Robert Frost.

On a Summer's Day in June

On a summer's day in June
I check each flower in turn
In my Garden of Delights.
Then I read some Robert
Frost, and my joy's complete.

I watch the many ants and
Count the butterflies
Flitting all about. Depression
Out of sight, I'm one
Contented soul. Profusion

In the summertime makes
My heart feel free. I am
Beside myself with sheer
Delight. One more coffee,
More of Robert Frost. Oh!

The joy! Happy summ'ry days
Are here to last. As I fondle
Every flower, I feel a ladybird
Upon my hand. My world
Stops awhile—for now. It

Stays as if invited here, and
I don't move at all. A compact
Life of comely dots rests itself
On me. I'm overcome with
Joy. I let the joy of angels rest
Upon my hand. Oh! Ladybird!
Oh! Ladybird! Geraniums and
Roses give me pure delight. An
Old man very happy now. Today
I am a happy soul. Maybe, after

All, no longer old and grey.
Observing butterflies, sitting
Silently and motionless. My
Garden is a treasure beyond
My wildest dreams, a boon

For heart and soul inside. It
Gives me all I need on a
Summer's day in June.

Full Moon

Composing phrases, words sublime
Fit for books the Muses read, is a
Task divine, no less. It takes up all

My time. I labour on, distractions
All around. Creatures from the
Nether world invite me out to

Play in fairy shady groves, but
I stay put to finish my poetic
Task. In the moonlight hours

They have much fun, but I am
Resolute tonight. I'm staying
Put. I'll compose sweet verse

For my favourite Muse. I wait
For her tonight. Tonight's the
Full moon night. The underworld's

Wide awake and stirring now. The
Birds they do not sleep. All of
Nature's on the move imperceptibly,

Creatures full of merriment. The
Moon, it rides the clouds—all's in
Ferment in the shady groves this

Blessed night of moonlit light.
Happy me! Oh! Happy me! May
This last for e'er.

My Legacy

When I have gone, no
Longer old and grey, my
Poems may cause my
Folks to say *He was a*
*Goodly ma*n and then
Go on their way.

I would love if it were
So, but time will tell—
We'll see. Ingenious soul
I'm not, simple soul I am.
May my reputation stay
Intact.

My Sister's Grave

To my sister's grave I come to pay
Respects 'midst tears and memories
Of olden times. My triplet sister's
Close to me in my older years. As I
Warm to my task against the
Harrowing Irish rain, I shake the
Sorrow from my brow—in fact,
I'll sing a song of love. Yesterday
Is but a thought away. Yesterday
When we grew up, yes,
Yesterday! Now the melodies we
Used to sing come flooding back
To me. One more saddened song,
And I can happy go. Give me one
More youthful smile, back I'll go
To my routine much refreshed
And dutiful. My triplet sister's
Grave does wonders for my soul,
As I brave the gentle south-west
Wind upon my happy face this
Time.

I Want to Love

Tonight I want to love the world
As I loved the world in my youth.
People, folk, are lovable deep down.
I want to love them to the end.

Hatred, bitterness are out. Those
Days are gone, the winds which brought
Them have now ceased. Love is sacred,
Happy, bright. The netherworld brings

Bitterness. I urge you, reader, don't
Go there. Stay with the loving, kind.
Look up the poets who made love
To those who would just read.

Tonight I'm going to love the folk
Who are crying out for love, who
Want to give what they receive.
Tonight's my night for love.

Pondering

Oftentimes I ponder the deep, deep
Mysteries of life—alone—
In the park, and in the coffee house.
If I ponder on my bed, I get depressed.

I love to be with people kind and
Extrovert. I have to feel the pulse of
Life, to ponder properly. This I do
With people who have time for me.

The rapists and the sadist do not
Ponder life at all. But I'm different.
I'm gentle, kind—loving to the end.
I want to find some answers in the round.

I go for tea with ladies from my church.
On mysteries we do reflect, gently and
With dignity. But not alone. The scones
And biscuits help the job in hand.

Escape I must from solitude—I am no
Trappist monk. I like the people round
About. They keep me solemn, sane.
They take me from depression deep.

I ponder always life's inscrutable,
Alone or in a group. Refreshed—it
Heals my soul inside. For I am prone
To negatives, if I don't keep control.

Ye gods! That I may ponder happily and
In company that's good, polite, and
Positive. Grant me seeds of contemplation
Now, and I'll be whole once more.

The Hawthorn Bush

The hawthorn bush is gnarled, bent
By Atlantic winds unceasing in
Severity. A lesson here for humankind
If only we can see. Sturdy, hardy in
Its frame, its motto is *Adapt*.

Home to birds and animals, it gives
Shelter to them all. It will survive
In poorly soil, it will survive them all.
I'm attracted to my hawthorn bush
And its mythology supreme.

In my walks in Ireland's wild, wild
Fields, I notice my sweet bush,
Upright and adaptable. I'm watching
Out for foxes, rabbits, and their kind. I
Pass beside my hawthorn bush and

Sometimes take a bow. Nature so
Delightful. Unlike me, it is so sturdy
'Gainst the wind.

The Sound of Falling Snow (3)

Others do not hear the sound of
Falling snow at all. I hear it
Clearly, though, through practice

Long and diligent.
Tonight, this stilly winter's night,
The fairies, sprites, and gnomes
Bolt to their liars as snow

Approaches yet again. They were
Playing, scampering among their
Kind, quite happily with me. My
Muse, entranced, joined in as
Well. Until their troughs and

Valleys began to cover up with
White. They too can hear the
Sound of falling snow.

Robert Frost (2)

Robert Frost—I like his simple,
Perfect lines. I am addicted now.
When I am low I read him
To upgrade my mood again.

These lines indeed upgrade me
In my manic ways. *Inspire me
More* I plead my muse, *I want
To write like this great sou*l.

*But this is Robert Fros*t, she says.
*Robert is unique. Don't get too
Ambitious no*w. And I relent,
Fall silent on the spot.

I plead the gods that I may
Treasure this man's writings,
Keep them close to heart. Oh!
Stay with me, dear Robert Frost,

Stay tonight with me.

Inspiration

I crave the gift of creativity
Both now and in the days
To come. It is a blessing rare.

Depends on hard, hard work.
Nothing is for free I know
Deep down inside.

Yet some are given special gifts
That they cannot buy. These
Gifts are nectar from the gods.

The gods—they choose their own.

Life So Cruel

Why, Oh! Why is life so cruel
To some amongst us on the way?
Dealt such an unfair hand, I probe
This urgent quest, as I wake from
Heavy sleep and slowly scratch
Myself awake. *Give answer to
My quest,* I plead the spirits of
The night.

No answer comes my way, alas.
No small hint before me now, so
I'm despondent, very much.
Depressed maybe—unease, it
Grips my inner being all day. I
Know my moods elated, sad
Moods too, sometimes. They
Emanate from complex dreamy

States. A complex process this,
For sure. Now I'm moody for want
Of answers certain, sure. We know
That we don't know. Why? Oh
Why?

A Troubled Spirit

I have a troubled spirit now—
Too many questions in the early
Morning light. Life, death, and
In between.

Should I join the happy crowd?
Or probe these questions
Troublesome? I opt for
Awkward questions.

My happiness is fleeting, and
Is skin-deep at best. I delve
Into the classics old in search
Of answers for my soul.

I get distracted all too soon
And fidget to relieve my pain.
I pray the gods for answers
Quick, secure—But to no avail.

Tormented soul, indeed. My life
Is one long torment, truth be
Told. My aim is nothing short
Of bliss itself.

Happy answers found at last,
I hope, I hope indeed.

Departed Souls

In the moonlight, on a cloudy
Winter's night, I commune
With souls who've departed
Long ago. The exercise is
Fruitful for my spirit deep
Inside. I am in touch with
Deeper truths this passing
Hour.

All to the good for me tonight.
On the morrow I will visit
Gravestones long neglected
Through long years. I whisper
Prayers—the ones I mutter every
Time that I pass here alone.
Rest in peace—yes, *rest in
Peace for e'er.*

The Naked Tree

A forlorn tree in wintertime
Probing greyish sky, I turn
My head and see it skeletal
Alone.

This tree provided dappled
Shade all through summertime,
Now mere memory. Sadness
Now prevails. Intimations of

The death of humankind. But
There it is, standing sentinel—
Alone, for months ahead, its
Yearly cycle now complete.

Leafless, friendless, sad,
Sad tale to tell before
The snow arrives. It
Makes me sad to see it

Standing naked through the
Wintry storm. Standing
Silent all alone. Reminds
Me of my fate: I too will die.

White Sheet

I dread the pristine whitish sheet
Staring back at me. I dread it
Each and every time.

With fear I whimper in the
Early summer light. I call
My muse but to no avail.

Nothing for it but to write
A little, then more and
Much, much more until

My job is done. Pristine
White sheets in my dreams,
Oftentimes, oh! Yes!

Uneasy, I wake up, all
Upset, and moody too,
Words, more words, and

Words galore—that's the
Aim inside my soul this
Moment of creation new.

Oh! White sheet, thee I
Dread, in sleep, awake, just
All the time.

White sheet, white sheet …

My Prayer

I cannot go on bended knee.
Arthritis sees to that. I want to pray
For writers' gifts within my soul
This starving hour. My paltry
Prayers are mumbled standing up
Instead. Still, the good Lord
Listens to my crying plea this
Pleading hour. I plea the angels
And the saints to gather strength
To plead on my behalf. I tell them,
Ask the Lord to grant me gifts so
I can pen such poems as would
Please my audience. I cannot do
This on my own. This I know too
Well. Gather everyone around and
Plead on my behalf this earnest
Praying hour.

Frost

A hardy frost outside—
Winter's grip has
Tightened fast.

The robin redbreast
Perched upon the fence
Looking all forlorn.

My home is cozy, warm,
And bright. Outside it's
A different tale. Gone is

Summer's bounty now,
And we simply have to wait—
Wait through winter long

And hard. Patiently endure.
I like a walk in hardy frost,
The crispy air inside my

Frame—that frame that's
Old and frail. I'm waiting
For the fuller light—a

Midday sun, maybe. This
Frost is not relenting, but
Deep down I'm at peace.

Coffee and a roll-up at
This early hour: my recipe
For peace. In spite of this

Cold morn.

My Active Mind

Amidst musings of eternal truths I spend
An hour just pondering Life's mysterious
Ways. I pen a poem—but slowly now,
After I have supped. Today I'm full of
Notions for a poem new, and active
Though my mind may be, I cannot make
It right.

Confusion deep within—too many
Truths impinge upon my inner self.
I try to meditate just now, but still
Can't get it right. Ye gods! Assist me
In my task, compose my mind, and
Let me be at peace.

To a Robin Redbreast

Oh! Robin redbreast!
Charmer of the spare,
Spare winter months,
You notice me. We
Stare each other out.
Until, that is, you do
Resume your footprints
In the falling snow. Cold
And famished, you peck
At all the food I've left
About for you. Yes, you'll
Survive this winter's snow.
We'll work as one, just you
And me. Again you freeze
And stare—if only you
Could speak. You give me
Such delight each and every
Time. Do come to me, depend
On me, and I'll depend on you
Through the winter long and
Harsh and white.

Death Wish

For I would want a wiser mind
To end my days in peace.
Distractions crowd about me
Now; peace is still too far away
In my old age. I want to sleep in
Tranquil bliss instead of
Nightmares, awful dreams, each
And every night. I want my muse
Nearby, to consort upon a grassy
Knoll, to compose the finest verse,
And then I'll die in peace. My soul
Is longing for the day when I'll be
Free from stress, depression, and
The like. They claw at me and
Cling to me, forever keep me
Bound. The truth may be that
I'll be free the day I breathe my
Last. I am a tortured soul, for sure;
This illness stalks my soul. Yet I am
Free when I do see my Garden of
Delights; it is my summer medicine.
For months on end I am consoled.
No longer is my soul inside longing,
Pleading for release.

The Squirrel

The squirrel on the garden fence,
So cute and agile as I watch,
Mesmerized.

Nature's on the move again, 'tis
Springtime now. No more wintry
Days and nights. The savage

Blustery storms relented now—
Months of sunshine loom ahead.
The squirrel senses all inside its

Hardy frame, as it bobs atop the
Fence and makes me happy in
Old age.

The Sound of Falling Snow (4)

I crunch the snow beneath my
Feet, it's snowing hard just now.
I'll settle in my coffee shop,
Enjoy my friends and be at peace
'Midst falling snow.

It's time to leave, but I stay put
To ponder and to wonder still at
Nature's wilder ways. I'll pop
Outside to have a fag. Then one
More coffee—yet again.

I am going nowhere fast this
Wintry afternoon. The pleasures
Of retirement are laid on just for
Me this snowy hour. A croissant
With my coffee warm is all I need

To keep my soul at peace, ready
To compose when I get home at
Last. Snow, snow: Fall gently all
The afternoon in fantasy supreme.
Fall just for me, and I will listen

To the sound of falling snow. This
Is my rare delight in wintertime.
The flakes keep coming now. I'm
At peace at last. I'm greeted by a
Wonderland just outside the door.

Crunching thickened snow, I'm
Happy deep within. I worry how
The birds will cope. I'll leave them
Food, yet ask if they will see it
Through the snow.

Oh! Keep on falling, whitish stuff,
Keep on falling just for me.

A Poem Being Born

Cradling in my soul and heart
A thought original, a poem new,
Not yet fully born. My mind is
Concentrating now. I am
Consumed with pain. There
Comes a time when poems
Emerge as if on cue. That time
Is now for me. This act takes
All my energies, and, word by
Word, my poem is born. The
Muse is midwife to me now.
Creative acts do take their
Toll. This poem exacts its
Price. I'm tired and weak—
Exhausted if I tell the truth.
My poem I fondle and caress,
Give it love and kisses too.
Slowly it responds, prompting
Me to add more words to help
It on its way. I love my poem.
May the reader feel the same.

Early Morning Light

I like when night has gone,
When morning's light has come
And we can see the world at last.

The searing light of summer sun
Upon an afternoon must yet
Emerge. No—this is gentle,

Early light as I survey my summ'ry
Garden patch. This light invites us
Out of doors to have a coffee at

Our favourite seat. A cigarette to
Settle nerves as we scratch
Ourselves awake. We survey all

That's there to see and feel the
Light permeate our being. This
Is not a time for bed.

Instead, we watch the birds and
Millipedes and check the garden
Plants galore, and in full bloom.

Oh! early morning light, you
Coax us slowly to a new-formed
Day. I am grateful to the gods.

Poets Unite

Lovingly and daringly I want
The world to sing a happier
Song this day. Our music is
Too sad this hour, methinks.
Let us raise our voices and
Our fists to make it clear
That we do care, that we
Are one with Nature, with
Ourselves. Discordant
Voices there will be, but we
Must these ignore: we must
Unite this day to save the
Planet where we live, where
We love, and where we find
Our inner selves. Poets of
The world unite and clench
Your fists—but lovingly and
Caringly this day. March as
One, lovingly and caringly
This day, this goodly hour.
We too are peaceful folk—
Count us in as well, I plead.
Engrave our names upon
The stone erected in the
Cause of humankind.
Engrave for sure, but
Lovingly and daringly.
Engrave for all to see that

We stood up, were counted,
For truly we did care and cared
Again when they came knocking
On the door. Poets come with
Roses, not with guns this sober
Day. Roses carried lovingly and
Caringly.

An Old Man's Beady Eye

Vulgar, haughty I am not
In my old age. I seek a
Life of pleasantness to
All I come to know.

I'm caring, kind,
Compassionate. I've seen
The opposite in my long
Life and know what it

Achieves. Instant death
Within, I'd say. I keep in
Touch with milder folk
Who spread the word of

Peace. I keep away from
Those disgruntled in their
Later years. My virtues
Have been won through

Many years of growth. I
Will not lose them now.
Slow to walk, but quick
To practice kindnesses

Along the way—extended
To the neighbours' dogs I
Meet as I daily trek. Why
Hold guns when we can
Hold conversions made to
Foster peace? Put the roses
In the guns, I say. Put the
Roses in the guns!

I Long for Africa

South Africa, South Africa, I miss
You so. Durban and Pretoria, where
Family and friends do dwell.

I'm thinking of the friendship and
The love poured out on me. I
Miss it all this reflective hour

Alone. Deeply held beliefs shared
Together in the blistering heat.
The jacaranda trees I do recall

This night. Pretoria at its best.
Durban by the sea. I am in love
With Africa, and always will …

My Loving Dog

He's still my best, best friend.
A Cavalier King Charles, no
Less. We walk the London
Streets, go to the coffee
Shop. He has his treats right
Through the day and night.
He cares, he cares for
Uncle John in his old age,
And does so with panache.
Never now alone again, I
Love my doggy friend to
Bits. I read my poems to
Him. I think he understands.
He's patient all the time
To me—never answers back
Aggressively. My Cavalier,
So beautiful and kind to
Uncle John. Unlike the
Doctors and psychiatrists
He understands me fully
All the time. He doesn't
Criticize. Companion to the
Last. Without him I'd be lost.
My best, best, closest friend.

Life in the Soul

Life in the soul is troublesome,
But I have to seek the truth.

A lonely inner journey, if
Honest I can be.

No peace, no happiness at
Times is all I know.

Pray, dear reader, pray for
Me, an older man. Pray

I'll find the inner peace I've
Looked for all my life.

Life in the soul: that it may
Make an old man happy
In his final days.

Visiting Family in Pretoria

In one week's time I'll fly to Amsterdam
To catch my plane to Jo'burg. I'll stay in
Old Pretoria, with extended family to
Love.

All excited now, we'll drink the wine of
Africa, enjoying company supreme. We
Text each other all the time, and now's
The time to kiss and cuddle close.

I care about my family out there, and
They do care for me. New friendships
Too, are on the way, I'm sure. Two
Weeks of sunny bliss, I'll write anew
And return all refreshed again.

Close family ties I care about, I
Monitor my friendships close every
Single day. I need these folk, and they
Need me as well.

What else is there in life?

Busy Writing All the Time

My days are full of energy with nothing
Left to do. It's short—the time that's
Left to me—so I must beaver on.
There's not much time I tell myself, I
Tell it all the time.

So I'm busy writing, reading too. I'm
On a high eternally, fuelled by coffee
And my fags. Life is good, too short,
Alas, for me.

I'll read some poems in public view
Sometime very soon. That should be
Nice, like last time in the evening
Light. Then home to write again,
Alone.

As I pen these words I see outside
The morning's gathering pace. Soon
My folk here will arise, I'll have a
Respite from the drudgery alone.
I'll get a little sleep at last, but only
For an hour.

Give me fags and coffee, give me
Parchment new to place my words
Upon. I need to write eternally. It
Gives me meaning in my lonely
Life. It keeps depression far away.

The Bare, Bare Trees

The bare, bare trees of wintertime are
Skeletal and gaunt to me this lonely
Hour. They gave me shady solace
When summer's sun shone warm.

Lonely against the wintry sky this morn,
They're mysterious to me, reminder of
Eternal truths. I hugged them during
Summertime, and now they're all alone—
Like me.

Giving shady canopies no more, why
Do they exist? In wintertime?

They stand freezing in the early
Morning frost and so for months
Ahead. Cold and spare they are,
Future harsh conditions will test
Their eerie silence.

Especially my chestnuts so, so
Close to me. These bare, bare trees
They make me nervous now, and
So I'll stay indoors.

The Mountain Roads

Give me mountain roads just one more time.
I'll walk them with pure joy, rucksack on my
Back.

Give me green roads, soft, soft underfoot,
And I'll be happy as a bird twittering high
Above. The highways to the inner man,
Consumed was I in youth by wild, wild
Places such as these.

I studied all such roads, and I felt free—at
Home. Give them back to me I plead the
Gods and cry. I'm certain they'll say no!

Sad this hour I've only got the memories,
Sad I'll walk them ne'er again. Those days
Are no more. Depression has set in, I
Fear. My green road led to mountain
Pass. My compass was my friend. My
Muse—she came along as well.

Without my maps and compass I would
Never have returned. Of this I'm sure.
Stormy days and gale-force winds never
Put me off. The one great joy was wind
Upon my face.

These rugged roads, they led me safely to
Secret places far from home, but now
It's finished and for good, I cry. Life is
Cruel to me today; life makes me older
Still. Mountain pathways were my joy,
Negotiating past the hardy sheep and
Ponies wild.

Scotland, Wales, and Ireland too I
Traversed in my time. Japan and
China came along, the Middle
East as well. Oh! Give me back
Those heady days, let me walk
The barren paths, and content
I'll be.

I need a miracle tonight. I pray
The gods to grant me one for
Just one day again.

Alone.

Cemetery on November First

I came to Torun, Polish city fair, for this
Nighttime festival of light. It's a freezing
Night, November time again. We're
Solemn now, susceptible to faith intense.

The crowds are out, braving nasty wind
To be with loved ones looking down.
Lights and more lights everywhere,
Votive lamps give solace on this starry
Night.

Muffled cries I hear at times. My
Attention is distracted by Siberian
Winds. I'm frozen and dismayed to
See this ritual, naked faith on show,
But know deep down within that
Loved ones do return.

Poland at its best tonight, a
Privilege of mine to share this
Solemn ritual. A special night for
Me, calling out for Grandma, sure
She's listening now. A woman
Good and kind, she gave me in my
Youth the little that she had. We
Miss her, now we go, relieved.

Write, Write, Write

I'm writing all the time, or when I can,
At least. The same for delving through
My library. Days and nights are full of
Such activity. And I'm enjoying it all.

Obsessed I am with writing books,
The work involved I love. Reading
I'm obsessed about as well. My
Nights and days are full of words,
Good and kindly words to motivate
The way ahead.

I write for love of it. But it's demanding
On my time, my health, I fear.
I pray the latter is pure fantasy.
Obsession pure and full of joy.
Long may the dream go on. Long
May I write, and write, and write.

What Poets Say

What poets say at dead of night
Is manna to my brain. I listen to
Each word for succour and support.
Cryptic poems don't mean so much;
I like direct debate.

I ruminate upon the message simple
And direct. It's with me through the
Day. Its influence never wanes. I
Need to know what poets say—in
Print or on the stage. They call me,
And I listen well.

What poets say matters when the
World is out of sync, as now. We
Need our poets to say it for us,
Repeat it all the time, gently and
Convincingly.

Bless the poets. Bless what poets
Say.

An Old Man Died

I heard an old man died just up the
Road. I realised he was my friend,
In my coffee shop each day. It
Touched me so.
He was a kindly soul who loved my

Poems very much. He'd fought in
Wars, decorated too. He had medals
In his drawer, and brought them to
Our coffee shop one day. I saw his
Medals, he saw my poems: We were
Equal then, I guess.

They found him in his bed. He'd died
Alone, alas. But we buried him with
Honours grave and grand. His grave
I'll visit on my walks, the old man
All alone.

The old man died.

My Postman

My postman knows me very well,
A young man kind, reliable. He
Brings me all my books on time,
Each and every day, by noon.

We struck up friendship long
Ago; it's lasted all this time.
Always calls me *Mr. Ryan*, and I
Don't object. I don't like
Formality, but he means well
For me, my age.

My postman is a saviour now,
I'd miss him should he leave.
Long may he move around
These parts, for we need him—
And such as he.

Spring at Last

My Lord! It's mild this morning in my
Garden of Delights.

I've waited all these months for such
A morn as this. There's a difference in
The air today I feel. Just think: There's
Months of this ahead for me, growth
And happiness supreme.

Months of ladybirds and creepy-crawlies
Too. I'll saddle at my table and devour
My many tomes in sheer delight. I'll
Have my friends to tea this springtime,
That's for sure.

Winter's damage needs a clean. I'll
Attend to that this very hour.
Delightful task indeed for me, now that
Springtime has arrived. Oh! The
Months ahead are full of promise now.
I'll steadily write while steady growth
Is all about.

No more the dark, no more winter
Storms so devastating to my soul.
I can't believe that springtime's
Here; I'll have to pinch myself awake.
Ye gods! That I may comprehend the
Change in nature wild.

My Son Revisits Me

My son arrives at Heathrow terminal
Three from Las Vegas, where they
Live. Delirious I am at the prospect of
A week together, delighting in such
Company refined.

So much to say and do, I'm on a high
These days. We'll sit and chat about
The little things that go to make
Relationships.

I miss my Martin, Daria too. But we'll
Catch up and gossip share in my
Garden of Delights. Skype is not the
Same at all; better face-to-face.

They'll read my poems as well,
Exchanging good advice, telling me
A better way to write. Thank you,
Son, for coming home. I'm no longer
Old, alone. I'm a young buck, writing
Better now, and thanks to my dear
Son. Forty years of age I am, not an
Old, old seventy alone.

The National Gallery

I visit just to spend an hour with Rembrandt
And the Dutch old masters too. As I get older,
I'm closer to this master of the darker hues.
Soon I'll view impressionists; a day will pass
Me by.

I'll break for lunch, a glass of wine, reflecting
All the while on Rembrandt's darker side.
I've got the catalogue online for added
Satisfaction when I'm in the mood. I buy
The dad's, and I am happy seeing my
Rembrants in my home alone while I
Compose.

Monet, Manet, and the rest give me added
Focus in my work. So much to see, enjoy.
Who'd want to sleep all day?

Humbug the Cat

We have a local cat that comes to me
In my Garden of Delights. I can't
Describe the pleasure gained as I
Stroke it slowly now. An interference
In my work, so some might say.
No, not at all, I say.

Humbug is a friend to all, full of catty
Wisdom for the likes of me. I give her
Milk and stroke her head, she's purring
All the while.

Composing

Composing in the early morning hours demands
Of me a sacrifice supreme. A tiring time, I need
My wits about me to offset the tiredness
Ever present after little sleep.

Originality is far away. My mind is slow to
Operate at full speed on the parchment
Now. But soon I hit my stride. My pen—it's
Working overtime. A useful first draft soon
Appears.

Composing—Oh! Composing! A complicated
Task while Humbug my sweet cat purrs beside
Me now. Inside I've brought her for her early
Morning milk, and she appreciates it so.

A mild October morn just outside my door,
Patiently I play with words to start my day
With glee. But words don't come that easily
For I am groggy so, bereft of easy wiles this
Early autumn morn.

This writing task is cumbersome so early in
The day. I'll stick at it, and hope my muse
Might visit me, then everything would change.

My Empty Page

Nothing worse than staring at an empty
Page alone.

It truly frightens me, makes me feel a
Stranger in my home. Still, I need some
Discipline to overcome a trauma regular.

No friend of mine, this empty page, I truly
Hate it in the early morn. It just stares
Back at me, insolence supreme. I then

Attack it with a vengeance swift, and lo! it
Somehow warms to me, for reasons I don't
Understand.

The page is under my command. I cosset it
And place upon it words so delicate and
Wise sometimes, it now becomes a close,

Close friend to be fondled and caressed
Again by me, the two of us alone. Soon
Our passion is consumed, and on the page

Appears a poem new and grand. A poem
Fit for all to read. Behold! My work is now
Complete, and I am deeply satisfied.

I Am a Loner

I am a loner, lonely now, in my study all alone.
I do not venture far away from my lonely house.
Instead I am content with books and cat for
Spartan company alone. That's who I am in my
Old age, a geriatric fraud supreme.

Fraudulent maybe, I cross the Ts and dot the
I's until my heart says yes to all my lonely
Work alone. Grant me patience to complete
The work in hand alone, and still I'll happy be
To stay a loner till I die.

Snow Flurries

It's cold enough to snow today, just flurries now
Outside. I want six feet of heavy snow, so we
Will have to dig and dig again.

No way to see this prospect come alive, resigned
I am to winter mild this year. Just flurries now
This famished hour, the weather's disappointed

Me. Who knows, December still might give us
What we want, and more. Then happy I will be
In my room alone.

Inner Peace

Inner peace I pray for every day. Frustration grows
Inside as I compose. Quite placid is my nature
Deep inside my frame, but peace eludes me all
The time.

This is a gift not given to all, a blessing sacred
From the gods. So many people go without—
I want to have abundance in my inner being.
It's not deserved, it's given freely from the

Womb. So much I've suffered in my life, I'll
Not now know this gift unique: Inner peace.

I Am Devoted

I am devoted to my craft. Day and night
I write, and read and write again.

An all-consuming passion now, things
Will never be the same. I hone my talents
Few, in the wee hours in my room, in my
Garden, in the sunshine grand.

My garden is my room outside. There I
Consort with muses close. The sunshine
Urges me along with tea and biscuits
And my fags. No abating my fond
Passion now! It's all or nothing in my
Garden of Delights.

I am devoted, ne'er will cease. The
Muses granted me this gift, which I'll
Not squander now. I'll practice day and
Night unceasingly. No longer I will be
Alone, for the gods examine all my work,
Then smile when they are done.

The gods and Muses have been
Good to me. Got more than I deserve.

Advent

Weeks, long weeks to go—no bells just yet.
Privation, prayer, and sacrifice ahead before
We sing our joy, the joy of baby born for us
In Bethlehem of old.

When it comes, the bells will toll, loud and
Cheery too. All will be invited round to see
The crib festooned with children's help, as
We inculcate deep mysteries inside those
Little minds.

For now, for me, it's hard work praying to
Mary sweet, a mother in the waiting. That
I'll be guided safely and not renege on
Promises made long, long ago. Promises
To keep the faith in spite of lapses in
Old age.

This is wintry Advent time, a lean and
Spartan time indeed. I slowly crawl to
Church to pay my dues and give respect.
I'll have to wait for Christmas glee.

I'll simply have to wait.

Monkish Chants

I play the monkish chants while I
Compose at times. Gregorian
Chant is my great joy. It helps me
Concentrate and gives me inner
Peace.

I need that peace, I need those
Chants, more so as I grow old in
My garret cold on frosty morns.
The best time is the early morning
Time alone. I treasure that time
Best.

The simple nature of the chant is
What appeals to me. Never-ending
Joy is mine as the early birds show
Up. A new day dawns, the chant—
It charms me in the early hours.
I am entranced. I concentrate.
The monks are up at crack of dawn,
Just like me here alone.

Three Fifteen

It's three fifteen. I'm in my stride and
Writing well. My background music
Sober, quiet, helps me concentrate
Upon the task in hand. True, a
Lonely task it is, but I'm a lonely
Soul searching for the truth in my
Solitary quest.

I'm playing Bruckner's sweet, sweet
Music. It helps enormously this
Early morning hour. Too early for the
Birds just yet, pure pleasure to look
Forward to with coffee and my fags.
No problem writing at this early
Hour, today. The gods are kind to me.

I'm feeling groggy as they've changed
My tablets yet again—no cat to keep me
Company. Where is Humbug when I
Need her most? Just to stroke her
Would be nice, but she is busy chasing
Mice, I guess. Nothing for it but to
Write, and write, and write again.

At three fifteen. Yes, three fifteen
Alone.

Happy Through the Night

Happy through the night am I
Composing, writing words and
Words and words again.

I beaver on, guided by my muse
Nearby. The starry night is cold
Outside, but I'm in my element

Just now, scents emanating from
My muse, her music soft and
Sweet. Writing times are hard

Sometimes, but not *thi*s starry
Night. Stay with me, muse so
Sweet and comforting. Forever

Stay close by, to guide my
Shaky hand, gnarled and old, alas.
My hands are like an old, old tree,

A noble chestnut past its youth.
They stop me writing, scrape the
Page. But I'm resigned to this.

May I stay happy through the
Night.

The Gods I Place on Notice

The gods I place on notice that they
Must help me now, to finish this my
Poem this morn. I'm stuck, I'm badly
Stuck, I simply can't proceed alone.
I'm low on inspiration, cannot find
The words fit for my muse and
Others of her kind.

I call upon the gods to smile on me
This hour, to write a poem fit to read
And able to inspire. My spirit's dry,
I'm not consoled one bit. Nothing
For it but to write and write and
Write.

Mesopotamia

How I'd love to visit there in my
Old age, to visit dusty ruins and
Scrape the dust off ancient brick
Just to satisfy my thirst for
Knowledge old, respected all
Along.

Too late these days, alas—too
Late. I cannot travel all that way
To see the places where it all
Began. Sumer, Indus Valley,
Too, and Egypt. Ancient
Pottery from Japan added to
The growing list.

Give me Tigris, Euphrates too,
To wander all along in
Reflection deep. Today we see
What writers wrote, we gape
And marvel all the time. The
Ruins are there to see, now just
Piles in places, so.

But not for me in my old age.
Not for me.

That Day in Old Saigon

That day in Old Saigon I saw a face,
A female face. I was rooted to the
Spot. Completely mesmerized was
I—a beauty such as I had never
Seen before.

My new-found *Mona Lisa* in the
Flesh, just selling trinkets in the
Market ancient there. To this day
I recall that face, I'll ne'er forget,
Not now in my old age.

I couldn't pass the time of day,
Much less a compliment. I was
Besotted there and then that day
In Old Saigon so many years ago.
She glanced at me so furtively,

She wanted me to buy, but my
Mind—it wished that I could
Paint her, paint in oils at that.
Those days I painted all the time,
But this was not to be.

Her eyes beguiling flashed again,
Eternity itself did pass in a moment
Swift in that dusty, sunny day. I was
Overcome by now. Discretion

Made me move along.
Move along I did, but just one
Final glance at her as my heart bade
Her adieu. I'll ne'er forget that face
As long as I'm alive. Forever I'll
Recall that day in Old Saigon.

I Take the Infant in My Hands

I take the infant in my hands
While it's fast asleep. My old,
Old shaking hands caress it
Gently so, and on it sleeps
The sleep of innocence.

Good therapy for a fogey old
And ancient now, I can't help
Wonder what her future
Holds. May she be gentle too,
Good and kindly to mankind

In a long, long life so happy
And so strong. May she know
Adventure, love, and peace
Deep down inside. Instinctively
I pray for her, for happiness

Supreme. I hold in my arthritic
Hands the future—nothing less.
A privilege indeed, at this stage
In my life. I thank the Lord for
This great gift today. Bless her!

November Gales

The storm last night—it woke me up at three.
I sauntered to the kitchen fast, made a cup
Of tea. A vicious gale was in full might, I
Stayed awake all night.

The savagery outside my door did shock me
To my inner core. I thought I'd seen it all
Before, but clearly not the likes of this.

I thought of souls way out at sea; memories
Came flooding back. Other times and places,
Yes, but this was here and now—a savage
Here and now.

From my front door I gazed upon one hardy
Fool, bent against the wind. Soaked right
Through, he battled bravely on. Retiring to
My cosy den I worked away on poems new
But was distracted by the fury of the wind.

November gales were ne'er like this, I'd
Thought—the thoughts of youthful nights
I'd spent camping in the wild came back to
Haunt me at this savage hour. More than
Once my tent was wrecked. I famished
All alone on mountaintops with my drop

Of whiskey by my side. This gale, it blew away
At last, evoking mellow notions now amidst
The newfound peace and quiet. Out I went to
See the damage done all night. Done it was all
Right. The rush hour was more muted now. I
Sipped my coffee in the shop, exchanging
Wordless glances to my left and right.

I'll ne'er forget this night. In years to come I'll
Reassemble the full might of all the damage done
And bid farewell to winter with relief at last.

Tashkent

I wandered through Tashkent,
Samarkand as well, across vast
Deserts in the heat, when I was
Young and travelling far.

Exotic places gripped me then.
My eyes saw architecture finely
Wrought. The women dressed
So colourfully—I was besotted,
Mesmerized.

I found the heat unbearable but
Determined to survive. Our
Guide I still remember to this very
Day.

On we went to Samarkand. I loved
It all, wanting it to never end.
A culture shock indeed, it sowed
In me a lifelong wish to travel
Widely before I die.

Now that I don't travel far, I
Do recall such destinations far
From home. They made me who
I am.

I Feel for All the Lonely Now

I feel for all the lonely now as they do
Grieve and mourn and pine for those
Who've gone before. I understand the
Pain, the loss eternal in their souls
Tonight. No relenting of the pain,
Nothing but that numbness deep,
Deep down inside.

November's graveside vigils make it
Even worse. Tradition must be done
This day, holding back the tears as
Ne'er before. Ye gods! That they may
Hold their peace and spirits fast—
That they will find the strength to
Bear the pain unbearable.

A final placing of the flowers, to do
The thing correctly now, seems all
That matters as they move on to
Other things and duties now.
Always they'll remember when life
Was sunny, happier, when smiles

Accompanied a loving face; but
Now the smile's the stuff of
Memories alone.

My Triplet Sister Anne

My triplet sister Anne, one cold January
Day you departed from this life, and we
Never said goodbye. You and I were
Very close, but now we're closer still.
We played our childish games in
Ireland's faerie fields, we were as one
While growing up, but now it is no
More.

You're buried by the trees in an Irish
Grave. I visit you and shed a tear; the
Pain is ever near. Life is cruel to me,
Dear Anne, I'm sure you understand.
Come home to me far, far away from
Pleasant, fertile fields and tell me of
The bond we have and that we
Always will.

I love you now, I loved you then, I
Always want some part of you to be
Inside my very being.

Especially just now.

The Sound of Falling Snow (2)

When we look out and see the falling snow
It gives us inner calm and peace just now.
No breeze at all, just stillness all around.
The snow reminds me of those days in
Ireland long ago.

I was a lad, just ten, absorbed by this
Phenomenon. At seventy, the fascination
Still is there. I gape and gape so
Endlessly at this miracle close by. My
Writing calls me to the page, but not
Just yet, I tell myself.

One more moment of this wondrous scene.
Now I'll write with added zest, rushing
'Cause I want to don my clothes and wander
In the snow. The greenery is now pure
White; the traffic beat the rest to slush.

Snow, white snowflakes, stay awhile. Fill us
With eternal calm, the peace that comes
From falling snow—the soul that's now
At peace.

Six a.m.

I've woken up, I'm groggy now, a busy
Day ahead collating all my thoughts.
My mind is concentrating on those
Folk who're settling down to write,
Like me, who do it so much better
Still.

Why? Oh why? I ask myself. I am
Denied this precious gift, languishing
In misery sublime, alone, bereft of
Comfort in old age.

They've got control of words and
Thoughts, they manage to endow the
Page and fill it up so easily. Not me,
Not me. But why again, I do
Complain. This craft is not for me, I
Sometimes think.

Poets from Across the World

I've invited to my study warm and bright
Poets from across the world, to sup with
Me and talk to me, motivate my soul
This cold and wintry night.

A veritable feast, indeed, I love these
Times when my house is full of glee. No
More lonely struggle—farewell the
Negatives. Instead there's inner joy,

Creative notions in my soul tonight. Good
Riddance to depression, be gone the
Dreaded dryness way deep down inside.
My friends the poets guide me in new

Ways, after which I am a better man, no
Longer lazy, old. Long may this last—for
This I plead in church. But soon these
Poet friends depart, more in haste than

Sorrow. And I am so relieved—uplifted
Deep inside. Thank the Lord for poet friends
Now I'm on a high. That it may last is my
One wish this cold and wintry night.

Ten Million Dewdrops

Ten million dewdrops on the hedge
Created overnight while mankind
Slept.

In brilliant sunshine I'm absorbed by
Nature's miracle. The sticky
Cobwebs will be burnt away quite
Soon. *How many will have noticed?*
I ask myself.

Tonight it will repeat itself—perhaps.
Tomorrow I'll be mesmerized again:
A never-ending cycle in my mind. I
Like December days like this, my
Writing's better from it all.

Closely look and count the drops upon
The leafy glaze. Be fascinated all the
Time. You will be a humbler man
Indeed, more wholesome in the round.

My Heart Is Upbeat

My Heart is upbeat in the brilliant sunshine
Now, 'tis good to be alive and active like a
Youngster, free.

Depression's gone, no more negatives alone.
Head down, I'll write and keep on writing
Till the lowering sun, no more shaking

Hands—my body's in good shape. *That it
May las*t, I whimper silently. Upbeat is the
Mood today; my heart's responding well.

Grant me mental clarity so I can pen a poem
Clear and good and not some rubbish fit
For the garbage bin.

Amen, amen.

An Irish Cemetery

The souls of those who've gone before
Lie here before me now. Atlantic gales
Have gnarled the trees, stunted growth
All round. But still there's fertile Irish
Soil. I meander all alone.

A deeply meditative trek this early morn
In May, I've come to greet my triplet
Sister Anne who now is laid in silent
Peace with just the whining wind for
Company.

The sky is overcast, clouds scurrying above
Me to suggest some rain quite soon. If I
Get drenched, all to the good—I've done
My obligation for my undying love. All
Is now at peace.

Nothing more to say.

Like a Trappist Monk

In my cosy kitchen I brew my coffee in the
Early morning hour alone, saying nothing,
Not even to myself.

I sip mindfully. In summer I have it in my
Garden of Delights. Now's not the season
For such luxury. I would be lost without
My first hot coffee sweet. I cannot get to
Grips with life's complexities without my
First warm coffee brewed.

I was a Trappist monk in another Life, I'm
Sure. To this day it's rubbed off on me.
My solitary soul is Merton-like: I
Contemplate the way things are, and
This is all the time. Seeds of contemplation
Grow within me all the time.

Forever I am claiming mountains of the
Soul, forever falling short for lack of
Training good. May I be guided in good
Ways, gently shown the way. But I need
My coffee first.

Making Poems

Rubbing hands on the dusty bricks of
Ancient habitations, instinctively I want
To write a poem—gently, softly.

There's something primal in making
Contact with souls who've gone
Before, and I am loving them and
Knowing them so gently and so
Tenderly.

But they are silent totally this
Reflective hour. Just like my triplet
Sister in her Irish grave. Yet we do
Speak the language of the dead.
Assuredly they hear our murmurs
And our fumbling through the
Eons.

Such times as these make me want
To write, and so in heart I mumble
Words and phrases brief. I will
Transcribe them later to be there
For all to know of my visit to this
Ancient place, now no more.

Arise! you souls, and shout aloud
About your ancient lives and loves
In this place remote. Speak!

I'm Committed

I'm committed to the writing task, scraping
Vellum every day. I'm up at dawn with
Coffee—work late into the night as well.

It's painful in my soul sometimes,
Decisions faced about my themes as I
Fumble on my tablet with the early
Birds for comfort then.

Companionship is rare in the early hours.
I beaver on alone, committed as I am.
A lonely life, so some might say, but not
So, I respond. I'm wrapped up in my

Work, avoiding all distractions now,
Getting thoughts on paper before the
Day's begun. I'm committed.

A Mild Winter's Day

Eerily mild in my beloved garden,
I sit sipping coffee warm and
See two squirrels darting to and
Fro. Two more hours of daylight
Left, and then I'll wonder why we
Have this break from winter's
Harsher ways.

But oh! The trees they look so
Gaunt and are stripped bare. No
More leafy views, alas. The
Chestnuts are so skeletal, poking
At the low, low sky in silent
Admonition, as it were. This is the
Stuff of milder winter days in my
Garden of Delights.

Shimmering Shafts of Sunlight

The summer flowers are full of glow,
Shimmering shafts of sunlight all
Around the place. It's early morn,
Busy birds twittering away, and I'm
Content this June day.

It's bright at half-past four—long,
Long days to dawdle in my
Garden of Delights. My coffee and
My fag, my books and tablet too.
Life is free and good to me.

The light, intensity, and brightness
Immerse me in mindfulness today.
Impressionist light this is—I reflect
What light we'll have by 2 p.m.
Geraniums, my favourites, are

Sending sap that I can hear, for I
Have ears for everything this early
Hour. I roll another fag in sheer
Delight, coffee long gone cold.
Distractions happy all around.

Oh! Lucky me.

Raindrops

Autumn time—the raindrops gently fill my
Window pane. It's very mild outside.

Today I'll slowly take some air, sip some
Coffee in my cafe near. I'll write and mix
With people kind, reflect on summer's
End so suddenly. I'll pat the dogs,
Especially my favourite Labrador waiting
Patiently for me.

How I'd love to have a Labrador, but I'm
Not allowed—too old, they say, too slow.
Oh! woe is me. Life is so cruel. It's now
Raining steadily, rivers running
Down the window pane. But I'm tucked
Up inside, busy studying raindrops.

The Lonely Folk

The lonely folk, forgotten now, are in
My thoughts this hour.

The world's too busy making cash, no
Time to wonder who and where they

Are. Once they lived and loved; now
They are alone. Loved ones dead,

Maybe, or far away from loving
Hearts. I remember all the lonely

Folk as I trek to church this freezing
Winter morn. They too deserve

Remembrance, deserve a special
Prayer from deep inside my soul.

Wild, Wild Winter's Night

Wild, wild winter's night outside, a soft
South-westerly hard at work creating
Havoc all around.

A mild wind nonetheless. The moon is
Riding high through all the clouds far,
Far above me now.

Summer's but a memory; spring is far—
Too far away just yet. We'll have to
Have the long, long patience of the

Hardy folk, who've been through

This before. But I'm impatient for
The springlike songs of birds.

This, in my Garden of Delights,
Budding springtime growth. But
This mild, windy night is just for

Brave, brave souls who venture
Through a vicious winter wind.
Not me! I'm staying tucked away

With much-loved books for company.
I cannot read with pleasure now: the
Scream upon the eaves is much too

Much to bear. A fag and coffee, then.
My doctor won't be pleased, for sure.
What else to do on wild, wild winter

Nights like this? I'll don my coat and
Take a walk and bear the brunt of
Hail and wind upon my face.

Soon I'll tire, and sleep right through
It all.

A Listless Morn

It is a kind of listless morn, this
Morning in the spring. The sun's
Not fully grown; the moon left
Far behind, the stars now faded
Too. Utter calm pervades my
Soul this morning in the spring.

I see a millipede and wonder at
Its charm. My mood then
Changes: Now I'm listless,
Suddenly. My medication makes
Me go like this. Nothing for it
But to write, and write again.

I spy an early ladybird, too early
For the butterflies. I tell myself
Be patient! And so I am in my
Garden of Delights.

Retired at Last

I've got to rise, but not for work. For
Forty years this was the case, but now
It is no more.

I am retired, My journey's to my
Garden grand, to simply dawdle in the
Early morning sun.

I hear the traffic but ignore it gladly.
Instead I listen to the birdsong overhead.
I concentrate on creepy-crawlies at

My garden table 'midst the roses damp.
The dew has soaked them all. I now
Indulge myself in mysteries to do with

Growth, and listen to the rising sap. No
More traffic fumes for me. I've retired.
My time is now my own.

Arcadia

I wrote a poem once. It simply asked:
Why don't folk hold hands
Instead of holding guns?

One Day at Work

One day at work a young man
Raped me savagely. I've never
Been the same since then.

Three times I entered Bedlam,
Three times I was allowed to
Go.

My daily dose of tablets keep
Me on a level each and every
Day. It will remain that way.

Flashbacks to that day are with
Me all the while. How cruel is
Life to those who're gentle, mild.

In the Springtime Park

In the springtime park I saw a youngster
Fascinated by the ducks. He proffered
Bits of food, waving hands excitedly as
Mum kept watch close by.

I stood there mesmerized. *Welcome
Spring*! I murmured deep inside, the
Boy completely unaware of my
Secret thoughts, completely

Unaware of me. I sat and concentrated
Hard, determined I'd pass by again.
I often do recall that lad, his splashing
Ducks. I was a boy again.

Daffodils and Snowdrops

In springtime in the local park I take
A measured walk. I'll have coffee and
A roll-up to beef me up for further
Prowls.

I feed the ducks, then wander further
On, past the daffodils and snowdrops
In glorious array. Such beauty in the
Morning hours creates in me a hymn

Of sheer delight. This was made for me.
Oh! Lucky me! I cry, then wander home
To write and write and write some more
In my much more modest Garden of

Delights.

A Poem

A poem is such a gentle thing,
Just like a spider's web in the
Summer morning light.

This, my poem, is from my
Heart. Treat it gently now;
It tells precisely who I am.

An offering for all mankind,
I give my poem to all who
Wish to know precisely

Who I am. Like me, it's kind
And kinder still, probing
Mankind's questions which

Disturb our inner souls.
Perhaps they stop us
Sleeping through the night.

Go to the world, dear poem.
Ask big questions if you must,
But ask them gently, gently,

Nothing more aggressive now.
Remember that. Don't disturb
The reader, mind—the reader

Has a disposition warm, full of
Expectation too. Treat the reader
With respect, kindly, gently too,
Dear poem of mine.

A poem of mine is full of kindness,
Full of trust and early-morning
Hope. May a poem of mine
Reside within the breast of readers.

At My Sunday Church

I notice at my Sunday morning church
An old, old man, deep in mystic prayer.
I envy him. I cannot pray like that.
Problem is, I simply cannot pray.

I'm fidgeting, full of distractions too.
Simple prayers get all mixed up with
New-found poems deep inside. I'm
Playing with words and phrases as I

Am supposed to pray. So I watch the
Old man near me and watch him
Closer still. He is a living saint in this
Bad, bad world of ours. I'm jealous.

I Get No Pleasure

I get no pleasure from my prayers
As I start my day from way inside
My soul. I'm not cut out to be a
Saint. I'm a pagan running wild.

The world is full of pagans just
Like me, I think sometimes.
Hard pressed, cunning, hardy
Souls: *Why bother?* I do ask

Myself. I get no pleasure from
My early-morning prayer,
Heartfelt though it be. Free me
From this dryness of the soul,

Dear Lord. I pray incessantly.
I've read the mystics but to no
Avail. *They're not kindred spirits,*
I do assure myself alone.

Stick to what you know, I tell my
Inner man. *Don't probe beyond
Your depth.* And so I do, this very
Hour. I get no pleasure, sadly.

Sadly.

My Geraniums

Gingerly and tenderly I cosset
My geraniums in the morning
Of the world.

They're hardy, tough, and do
Respond to my every touch.
Apart from roses, they're my

One true love in this Garden
Of Delights. I'll grow some
More this year to make my

Pleasure more secure. *Keep
On greeting me*, I cry. *Keep
My Heart forever young!*

They tolerate neglect and
Drought, but on my
Windowsill there's such a

Treat for all my neighbours kind.
I get the compliments from
Strangers now as I stand at

My front gate smoking,
Sipping coffee too. It makes
My day, for sure.

Deep Inside My Being

Deep inside my being there's a yearning
For a fuller sacred life. The poets
Gather round my bed as I lie ill at home.
Heaney, Milosz, Szymborska, Platt—and
All the rest as well. Not room enough
For all of them tonight.

Deep inside this frame of mine there's
A longing to go out and face the storm
Raging all around. But I'm too ill to
Move. Seventy, and not a decent poem
To show for it. *Dig for me, Mr. Heaney,*
I cry out, a tear across my wizened face.

Deep inside my sober soul this night, I
Plead with proper poets to share their
Gifts with an old man in his bed, awake.
I need a sacred inner life. I plead with
Gods and muses to grant me this last
Wish—to make an old man happy now.

Enough!

There's a part of me that says *Enough!*
When I try to ape the greats.

I should be just myself, humble too,
Not negotiate the heights I cannot
Reach.

These are swampy lands 'round here.
Sometimes I'm stuck and cannot get
Away.

Enough indeed, I know—ambition is
The enemy lurking just beneath my
Skin.

Follow in the footsteps but not to
Strictly imitate. Take a look at
Robert Frost, and leave well alone.

Oftentimes

Oftentimes I wander through my life
And wonder what I have achieved,
What to follow on from here,

I read the classics but to no avail. I
Ruminate and masticate, ask
Awkward questions of myself, and

Still no answer by the time the sun
Has set. I go to bed dissatisfied, an
Old man so disgruntled now.

What have I achieved? Does it
Matter now at all? Some rubbish
Poetry, perhaps? Where grand
Visions of my youth?

Yet, I am loath to simply leave
This life without a legacy.

The Gypsy Melodies

The melodies that haunt my soul
Are Gypsy melodies I heard in
Munich's streets.

Stories sad, melodious, they
Struck a chord then in my youth
A long, long time ago.

In my old age, give me Gypsy sad,
Sad song, sung by that blind and
Chastened figure, famished by

The cold. I do cry now, as I cried
Then, forty years ago. The hairs
Do rise upon my neck when I

Listen one more time to
Timeless Gypsy melodies. I
Proffered pennies in the hat.

The violin was all aggrieved that
Afternoon in Munich ancient, far
Away. Sing one last time for me.

I Want to Tell a Story

I want to tell a story, a tale from
Far away. A tale about my life and
Loves, so painful in the telling now.

Little room for happiness, no
Room at all for merriment. A story
Full of sadness to this very day.

But still a life fulfilled. The latter
Years were happy, more so than
Before. My soul matured, I saw

Some truths clearer than before.
Retirement was a boon, for sure.
My life's now run a full course

Steady, sure, these last few years.
This is my story brief and true.
Sting in the tail, maybe.

My Triplet Sister's Grave

To my sister's grave I go to pay
Respects 'midst tears and memories
Of olden times.

My triplet sister's close to me in my
Older years. As I warm to my task, I
Shake the sorrow from my brow.

In fact, we'll sing a song of love.
Yesterday is but a thought away.
Yesterday—when we grew up,

Yes, yesterday! Now the songs we
Used to sing come flooding back to
Mind. One more song, and I can

Happy go. Give me one more
Youthful smile, then I'll go back to
My routine much refreshed and

Dutiful. My sister's grave does
Wonders for my soul as I brave
The south-west gentle wind upon

My happy face this time.